LITTLE HOUSEWOLF

Little Housewolf

MEDRIE PURDHAM

THE POETRY IMPRINT AT VÉHICULE PRESS

Published with the generous assistance of the Canada Council for the
Arts and the Canada Book Fund of the Department of
Canadian Heritage.

 Canada Council   Conseil des arts
for the Arts   du Canada

SIGNAL EDITIONS EDITOR: CARMINE STARNINO

Cover design by David Drummond
Photo of the author by Rae Graham
Set in Minion and Filosofia by Simon Garamond
Printed by Marquis Book Printing Inc.

Dépôt légal, Library and Archives Canada and the
Bibliothèque national du Québec, second trimester 2021.

LIBRARY AND ARCHIVES CANADA CATALOGUING IN PUBLICATION

Title: Little housewolf / Medrie Purdham.
Names: Purdham, Medrie, 1974- author.
Description: Poems.
Identifiers: Canadiana (print) 20210111003 | Canadiana (ebook)
20210111038 | ISBN 9781550655674
(softcover) | ISBN 9781550655735 (EPUB)
Classification: LCC PS8631.U73 L58 2021 | DDC C811/.6—dc23

Published by Véhicule Press, Montréal, Québec, Canada
www.vehiculepress.com

Distribution in Canada by LitDistCo
www.litdistco.ca

Distributed in the U.S. by Independent Publishers Group
www.ipgbook.com

Printed in Canada on FSC certified paper.

CONTENTS

For my family

Hinge

And that was our domestic cliffhanger,
to see how long that gate of theirs
would yawn and dangle on its hoarse hinge.

It was like a buccaneer who'd been told to walk the plank
but had caught the platform with one hand on his way down
and was just waiting to climb back on board.

It kept us on edge. We watched it every day,
coming home over the back field from the mines
to the row houses, where that one gate sat on its slant,

always swinging one-handed on its branch,
creaking monkey laughter
while the air turned sweet and spores grew hungry under our feet.

And every day we came home from over-the-way,
every day at the same time. Each to his identical little plot
piled high with long mouldy hay and lost plumage

and wondered if this would be the day the gate fell.
It belonged to a family of four, faces like Easter Island statues—
maybe they thought they could last it out.

Think of the relief, though, of letting it fall,
letting the blooming stalking pasture spill over between the posts.
letting the neighbours make the joke about finally coming unhinged,
sinking into the great, glowing, famished field, its undertow.

Carapace

Beach crabs, gleaning: you can hear
the snick of their victories, everything
jumps. Let me show you this one's underpanel—
just slide your thumb in right there—
this keystone piece in the middle, leathery,
is called the apron. Okay. Put it back.

Like a wound still charting its own outline, crabs
spread and settle their collectivity on the sand.
You remember our grandmother's foot
as she fried our breakfast, pocked just like this
under the oil's jubilation, and we saw

that one red claw grapple with her shin.
Her flesh tented and collapsed,
simmered red. She neither treated it nor
bandaged it, just put on her stockings,
where the wound was a live, fresh catch,
squirming incarnadine in a nylon net.

Otherwise odd about her wrinkled flesh,
she played with her arm's loose clothing,
an origami artist keen to demonstrate
mountain and valley folds. *Do you want some
skin? I have extra!*
              *I'll trade you
some skin for some height!* she regularly
propositioned our tall friend.
Guys. Your grandmother's offering me her skin again.

But the wound was hers alone; she covered it.
Did it sear itself there, or blend, an unremarkable
landscape? Even sand liquifies, unmindful
of its granularity: did her scar ebb, retreat?
Did her body ever grow forgetful
of the crepes with candied pear she served us?
Had we hung our heads to lift them to our mouths?

If the apron of the crab is rounded, like this,
it's a female. By law, you must let her go.
She'll disappear back to the home that
calls her, when its lithe incursion comes.
There she goes. See, now it has her:
mare, the sea, al mar, le mer, das Meer.

Bear Room

His bears were several, my grandfather's:
two big grizzlies, a small black bear,
one on the floor and two on the wall,
with heads on hassocks. Moose antlers,
hide. A wolf, a lynx, a chamois,
something else I cannot name,

deer family. A furry basement room,
big fireplace, dimmer switch, green bulb
transplanted and weird. Little, I worked the bellows,
endlessly changed the light. Inherited, in time,
the lynx, the chamois head, even the rifles.
They came to us in my late teens, in boxes,

like all mythic death waiting under wraps,
the Bear Room vestigial. As a child in that room,
though the oldest, I was the most afraid,
the finest fear when lit. Such a second retina I had
as a muskox has, animating forms in green light:
a live and luminous animalia, phosphorescent, angry.

Wretched with grief on the day Opa died,
I worked this exposure: I brought a friend to the
Bear Room, and when it stopped him cold,
I lost that clarifying eye, those figures.
("Have you ever been downstairs in this house?")
"My God," he whispered, looking around.

"I know," I said, and my voice wigged out
like any living thing's, caught by the scruff.

Painted Turtle

It was the size of a toaster, flamelicked
on the side like an ironic dragster,

broaching the yard with a plying gesture
with the air of something coming late to love.

When we lived on the ravine, dazzling things
would light upon us like metaphysical possibility:

a moth as wide as your palm, a pure-eyed mantis.
The quiver in the cedar of an unknown this or that.

The turtle went so far as to pose for a photograph,
as none of the others would. He looked pickle-brined,

questing and stolid. He said something, snoutishly,
about his purpose, disdained my childhood,

declared his solidarity with the material animals,
especially the marked ones, left in his own

                                        sweet time.

Bower

1. MANTIS

A loss to musical comedy, this leggy heir. See
  the way he approaches—angular, listening
behind stalks, making no move. How
  Gilbert and Sullivan would love him,
would set bright moths about him, would
  hear music in his arms' stuttering saws.

A loss to tragedy too, shield-faced thing. He's
  a set of futile wrists when the spider
wraps a breathless being, stiff as a
  cholera victim on a burdened bark,
jaw twice roped. He stands where we left him,
  silent, stumped, and oversees

the tying-up of ends. Look how each leaf is stippled
  with someone's thousand children, all identical,
some sucked from their husks and some not:

  this can't be anything but a garden of absent griefs.
Its prince drinks from a dewdrop without breaking it.
  This is only a grooming, this rubbing of hands.

2. DAMSELFLY

She swerves late, a teen new to driving,
    and the dew gessoes the tip of one wing.
        She won't make the lacrosse team now,
            think the golden scouts, rising in the stands.

3. MILLIPEDE

We curl into ourselves.

The humans engage each other
with novelty rings, strict
$1 spending limit. Hers is
a fat bulb of glass, painted
on the inside. Red and white
marble themselves convexly
through the glass like a prosciutto
sunset. His is a dragon
ourobouros, too big for his finger.
Its ominous self-devouring is
always on a tilt. On the resto
terrace where they sit, where
we curl, a man in a fedora
twizzles a rain stick for an
unlikely length of time. When
rice laughs, it sounds like our steps.

Imagine this guy is saving the world.
Imagine that if he stopped doing that,
a crevasse would open up right here,

says the man. True, thinks the woman,
this could be the millipedal music of
unscuttled civilization, the sound of circles

succeeding against being ovals, exerting
whatever force they have against
their own clattering to the floor.

4. BUZZ

August canola
gets its broadcast. *Is stone a
hero?* the son asks.

Hero? the son asks.
Wasps make a crepe dress, but the
father cuts it down.

Father cuts it down
like a wench from a scaffold,
with pity. Or some.

With pity, or some,
colour pervades everything:
between hues, noise.

5. MOSQUITOES

died vastly under the porch light,
if smoke could pile, a pile of smoke,
if thread could shimmy and fleck,
if the word licketysplit were carnal,
this would be that.

The husband still has them,
desiccated in a mason jar seven years later:
the slenderness of their lives, the radical
interruption of their feasts. Tiny, they were.
He wants to make art from them, he wants
to spray them with glitter. Gilded Bloodsucker,
he wants to call the piece. No, wait. GLAMPYRE.

6. OLD HIVE

It will be found in a different season from when it fell:
after the scaled-down insect tiger in the grass moves on,

long after the boy runs into the screen door
and the father says, "Caught one!" to the laughter of others,

after the snails approach each other in lobey love,
and the leaves shake off drops gelid as eyes,

and the bee settles into the petal canoe, ruffled undertaking,
and the thorn stops the turning of the dung beetle's globe.

It will be found after the world gives in to the point of the hummingbird's
proboscis and all the tiny skewed parasols are raised against the sun.

Someone's hands will skim over the comb, its emulsified
goblets; someone will show their child, and their child's friends.

What scraps are left in the dry compartments are clothes
donated to charity, in bags on the step,

and the husk will give itself then to our stiff fingers.
It will be as though we've never touched anything

from the garden before, nothing so forlorn. Everything follows:
the small, horned beetle at whose bonnet the child rejoices.

Look! Even the triceratops is not dead.

Kitchen, Vicarious

The summer that dolphins were found to have a self-concept, I housesat.
I read about them, turning before the glass,

in a house that remembered the forties.

Cut loose in wide rooms, I swooned over surfaces.
Look! *I have appliances*! I had space and furniture and corridors,
a plangent German piano. I folded my hands at a rolltop
desk, lost a needle in an upstairs room.

The resident cockatiel faked an illness; we made eye contact for an hour.
She lapsed first.

But the obliging cetaceans slipped and sidled.
Then, with a biologist's paint stroke on their backs,
they squirmed to scrutinize the mirrored mark.
I don't look like that! they were presumed to think.
Behind the two-way mirror, exultation.

Time stretched itself between borrowed walls.

I put some of the bird's millet on my fingernail,
venturing a bite with my gaze averted.
I waited for mail. In a classical mood, I spun down hallways,
sized up photographs: a child on a gate; a market pig,
square as a sideboard; a Salvage Campaign Queen
—somebody's relative?—colourized after the fact.

Crowned in a piece of twizzled scrap, she was Rockette-cheerful,
holding a pyrite sceptre ornamented with wingnuts,
bolted fast. Her suit, smart grey, made her a satellite
to the mountain of virtuous scrap behind her.
Its austerity gave my self-sufficiency game its loft.

At six o'clock, the televised dolphins were stymied again
by the glass, by their changed pearlescent bodies.
Could I do my hair in victory rolls? Could I learn canning?
Slowly they turned, true to themselves once more
soaking up the company of their own reflections.

Tooth

Her own tooth she found
secreted away in a drawer,
a tithe to something.
The clasp on the box
was another faulty bite,
a bottom peg and a top peg
that fell side by side.

Hollow as a seed pod,
the 17-month incisor could
be crushed between
two fingers. No good
for a fang necklace.
Sowed in the earth,
it would raise no army,

but it understood well
the shock of the precipitous
fall, its base jagged
as candied tatting. *So
much blood, and your
father couldn't take it!
His perfect little girl,
ruined.* Not like the hair,

which fell by design
into envelopes, taped
into books. The tooth
box smelled like chess
pieces, the hair book
like a meadow. One
day, she could be, like a
student meal, reconstituted,

if only to revisit down the line
her childhood accidents,
or so implied the tooth.
But then there was
the hair's own record,
written in the first of
her life's gardens: how much
sun, in the sundress
summer days, she took.

Binge-Watch

Nippy and coastal
crumpled world, we're here again.
When does evening start?

Semiquaver bird,
stone. Prolific actor—no,
doesn't matter who,

or, yes, maybe it's
exactly to the point, his
imprintable face.

That consternation,
those dainty teeth, even that
crisp run and close crop:

an adult form for
my lost school friend, these roles a
banquet of futures.

Nine seasons in two
weeks, one in five hours: that's how
I hustle his time.

He ruins so much
by saying *umbilical*
in the British way

but not before I've
seen all those filmed years
bristle, govern him

as they hadn't my
friend, who in so few seasons
passed beyond knowing.

The Tilled Field

What the sowed earth gives up is fair exchange.
        Things sprout up isosceles, in deference to the spade:

the saw-toothed leaf and the long tine of the tree trunk,
        the homestead's roof and the varieties of thorn,

all the lean pediments and the lines of balance.
        The weather-vane sits on its apex, unmoved,

till on the mead the lank sway-bellied mare drops her young,
        a crick-spined foal curving into his thirst,

till from the ploughed earth, the wanting hares come up long-eared
        and there are wavy implications of an underground twinge,

till the cry for sustenance is new and pointed, keening along lines.
        A fantastically-crested lizard emerges undertold from a tin.

And finally a human outburst of flags, climbing for the sun.
        The masthead of the folded journal shouts JOUR

and all the morning, tilled, is a composition of fallow land,
        the original hunger of animals, domestic things newly on the line.

The Thimble's Bucket List

To be a bucket. Like a housecat to a sabretooth, like a leaf to a canopy: to grade up. To contain—yes!—an abundance.

To cap the digit of a falconer's glove, to anchor flight's first maneuver. To be needled by nature.

To be ornamented. To be indistinguishable from a crown in bird's-eye-view, a trick of scale. To be stolen by a magpie. To line a nest, and to be overgrown there, sighing *so much for the monarchy*.

To be the subject of a child's brass rubbing, metallic pastel on black.

To play a shell game with two others and a pearl.

To be the mortar to a pinch of cure.

To line the keyhole of a piano, to resonate. To name a note as the threshold of all trembling: say, the middle b-flat. To know the child prodigy who played scales with one hand while catching flies with the other, stuffing their bodies into the keyhole. To be exactly that carnivorous. To be carnivorous to music.

To be lost while on a picnic. To stand empty in a crosswind, whiffling.

To decorate a sundial, pepper the light in a garden. To learn increments of time, finally, that are not seconds.

To visit the Bayeux tapestry, reading the linen from the finished side. To see the horse, the hawk, the man, the war, the conference, the king, the fording of rivers with shields held high over heads.

To defend the storyteller. To let her put her hand in the Mouth of Truth and not mind the scorpion.

To jamb the torturer's tong like a stone in the beak.

To fence, knowing intimately the poignant strategies of the foil.

No, instead, to work.

To settle into detail. To work a dorset-wheel button, spoked with a hundred stitches. To keep revisiting the centre. To be touched again, again, again, again, again.

Elisabeth

Ried-im-Innkreiss, Austria

After all this time, only this story remains:
you and your brother, tied back-to-back
for some misdemeanour, cast out in the snow.

Not Hansel and Gretel, not babes in the forest, not
felt-hatted foundlings of the Wailing Woods
in dimity dress: all cleverness, all distress.

It was the 1880s. If Chekhov had seen you,
he would have been as accurate about your suffering
as a chemist. *A littérateur is not a confectioner*!

If you had been Queen Victoria's children,
she might have made fond sketches of you from behind.
She was in love with small, retreating heads.

What happened to the punishing parent, the ropes,
the name of the brother that nobody remembers?
Were they nothing more than the flocking snow

nettling the naked ears? Could I gather into myself
the grain and scent of an Innviertler winter, make
the air sharply particulate, scuff the shoes and

know what you said to each other as your wrists
keened? Weren't you life-sized in the snow?
I think of little fallen ones, wizened robins, sheaves.

Ludwig Koch's Library

1. NEW PHONOGRAPH, EDISON WAX CYLINDER

How strange! Like a trumpet lily on a scaffold. His father's gift
from Leipzig: a beast-ear, a parliament, a fairy-skiff.

A voluntary bird drew close to sing its myth
into the wax. A shama from the child's zoo, its gift

was a florid arpeggio, a doodling recitative:
the world's first recording of birdsong, a fatherly gift

from an eight-year-old boy to humankind. Even Liszt
had met the child whose mind saw equal gifts

in the composer's art and the carrion-crow's cracked riff:
a field-appassionata or a fauve-salon. A father's gift,

it seems, is always wax and feathers. But if
a son doesn't know what to make of it?

His dread making no gift

of the sound, Koch's first military act was to play stiff
notes on a glockenspiel. In the thirties, *life became diff-*

icult, though his nature library grew. A whiff
of the future and he winged it to England,

and heard Brahms's only recording, the terrible drift
of white noise cut into the decaying cylinder, while the gift

of those personal bashing chords flayed themselves
into history. A reverberation is a tidal gift,

throwing itself forward into the harbour of other ears, list-
ing towards love. But records are always records. *Diff-*

icult, Koch wrote, *because we had been outspoken about
Goebbels, the long-tongued*. Though he found the gift

of new territory, his songs were lost, those waxen gifts.
The record skips, it skips, it skips, it skips

skips

The year I was born, so were Pong and the Rubik's cube.
The atoms were rehearsing a dire play in India.
Ethiopians were in civil war. A shark was no opportunist.
Argentina was extravagantly on fire, Nixon
withheld his tapes and I'm forced to admit
that the photographs of my lumpy bathing have long
looked historical though I'm not yet forty.
I would call that fact aesthetic, resting in
those tones, that matte, those rounded edges,
and the clock whose face was a trio of citrus fruit.

Soundless is the movie where my grandmothers,
who had only recently met, fiddle mutually
with my bonnet in swift gestures that
undo each other. One wants me to have
a bit more shade; one wants my face recorded.
It's a fishing trip, and someone is sneaking up
behind his mother with a frantic trout,
They're all quickening in the beached canoe,
to the fish's sine-wave thrash. The silence
is anachronistic for a year of celebrated tapes.
Lemon-lime-orange. Everybody's smoking.

A man named Ludwig Koch had died that year,
after an illustrious career with the BBC:
the year of the fuzzy seat covers in the Impala,
the Marimekko canvas in my parents' room.
As a child, he had played violin for Clara Schumann
and had recorded birds, made posterity

an avian thing. He died the year I was born. Who spoke
in Clara's ear speaks directly in mine. Phonograph
to Impala, Schumann to me, the war of the
Romantics thrumming through all of us,
all the affections and rivalries reverberating
somewhere, even through their silent recording.
It's possible that the bonnet itself is still worn,
untroubled by the disputing hands of love.

3. PHOTOGRAPH: MAN AND TRIPOD, OPEN FIELD RECORDING

Dear Koch: In your wading boots, with your high stand

at the moment of nightfall, in your greatcoat,

you're an overdressed Marcel Marceau with an

unexpectedly concrete prop.

I should have realized. It is all anachronism,

grasses vintage wild.

A fondness in the lit face, a hovering.

All ears are lonely. I know someone who collects only

music with "scene" in the title—

Kinderszenen, Gesangscenen—

she says she wants to walk into the songs

as through her own front door.

You are at home, gentle man. Your book

      told me how you stayed at the Savoy

where a kestrel had also been:

Kestrels do not build a nest: they just deposit

      their eggs in any suitable hole or nesting place, in this case

at the feet of an angel. The hotel cherub.

The sound of the newborn, the sound of the

      mother feeding it, the sound of the struggle

for dominance, the love songs, the answering love songs:

these are what you describe as the sounds of Paris.

      Chaplin, bird-perfect mimic, came the next day to the Savoy

but for you the kestrel with the predilection for angels

was the celebrity. Your microphone connects to something

outside the frame. You lean into the sound: it's everywhere.

(The barred owl says—my child loves this—

Who cooks for you?

Who cooks for you?

Who cooks for you?)

Poison Garden

It's the current Duchess's other garden:
        the banegarden, the slumbergarden.
                Who hasn't dreamed of being felled

by a plant? The first Duchess was a collector, got
        Cromwell's nightcap and Gloriana's satin glove;
                she opened drawers gently and wrote everything down.

The current Duchess doesn't stitch madeira hems or
        know the effects of the fly amanita; perhaps she races cars,
                plays foozball in the library when the visitors go home.

The poison garden is open for the August tours, where
        the poppy's tight and varicose bulb weeps
                at its own plush tracheotomy. None

of these Duchesses is the last Duchess, but yearly they tend
        the garden of her final weeds, water her lenten rose.

Newcastle Criminal Gallery, 1871-1873

Tyne and Wear Archives and Museums

In for thieving. For false pretenses. For more thieving:
Money, boots, a donkey, another donkey, more boots
and clothing. Their own coats (buttons all missing) pinned
on freak diagonals. Tweed coat stretched untenably across
a growing boy's stuttering and unfixtured chest.

For the record, they've never been photographed before.
But you can see that.
                              Old James Roman
(with his conqueror's name and his rococo sideburns)
hasn't had the art to compose himself. His eyes
are like Hadrian's wall upon the moor, a candid ruin.
No, they're like the space Hadrian's wall had wanted
to contain.

Mary Kirk: two months in Newcastle Gaol
for thieving. Doughy, and an ancient thirty,
she is—says her sententious photograph—
finally caught.

Luke Grieveson served four months in Newcastle
for a pigeon-stealing gambit. His necktie settles into
his waistcoat, its own maculate quail. The photo
is lightly vignetted, and Grieveson is listed as a clerk:
born in the city, grey-eyed, single and twenty-one.

Helen Workman, just eleven, *she's* a hard one. She
could be sitting for the constable or flying on a trapeze.
Sent down by the magistrate for thieving iron
with Rosanna from over the road, her eyes
show a relish for her seven days' hard labour.
No worse than the work I been doin' for me mam.

~

neon now, they flicker (scrubby girl, spare man /
scrubby man , spare girl) around the solid things
that were not theirs:

>   –two bob
>   –wool coat

Work-

>   –wrought iron
>   –ive poultry

>   **man**

>   –shoe leather
>   –fresh linen

Grieve-

>   –black boots
>   –rock dove

>   **son**

Tyne and Wear

LETTER FROM GRANDMA

Just a few lines to thank you
for your most welcome letter sorry to
have kept you waiting but never mind pet
I have getten there in the end.

When we were sparrowtailed banners
dangling from her laundry pole
wearing triangle scarves on our windy heads,
riding her palomino gate shut and racing in the street
(*Fall down? Eee, you should fall up next time.*
Never mind pet. Never you mind.), she was the trip
up the shops and the small bridled horse,
the hokey pokey on Lime Avenue,
the lollies from the ice man and the November bonfires,
the night bus in pyjamas, and the 50p
found in the field on the way back, for the 10p
lost on the way there.

Well it is Houghton feast week end
the Carnival was on Saturday
but it has done nothing but Rain
all the weekend and it has Spoilt everything
and it is still raining and it has to rain
all this week and you just get sick of it.

Riding out the echo of how it used to be,
when the pits were still open and all the bands came up
over the miners' bridge for the Durham Big Meeting
and you knew everybody. Dad bounced
his cricket ball off the coal houses and slung
pebbles at the milk cart horse to make him
tear off. My aunts practiced curtseys for the Queen
and Emily jumped laughing over the gate
to avoid a hiding. You heard the trumpets playing
from the pit bands, all the streamers trailing.

Sandy is going strong I think
he is about 8 or 9 years old now
he is still a good Barker lets everyone
know he's there. Well he has to go to the Vets
on Tuesday poor little soul to have
his tubes cleaned. I will close now
so I can get this off.

Suddenly everything on the telly was *crap*.
It's been those same two blokes. They haven't moved.
And Auntie Annie got robbed in her house by two
courteous thieves who made small talk with her while
they took everything she had, which wasn't much.
What was she going to do, she was in her nineties
and hadn't left the house in several years. And the two
thieves got off, like they said in the film, the blokes who
waited under a tree, talked about hanging themselves,
nattered back and forth and never moved
the whole time. That whole time. Well, never mind.

Well pet thats all for now till I hear from you again.
Hope we are not long in seeing you all again.
Could you give me your Code and Number
and the best time you will be in so
we can have a bit chat would be nice
hearing you again.

My answering machine deceives her when she calls,
not being in my voice, or revealing my name.
Her message says "But I *dialed...*" and breaks off.
But as a struck tine always shakes
the same song from itself, her voice
is the tra-la-la on the way to the shops,
the wind behind the door, the confluence of rivers,
the reverberation of morning bells and hillside green,
the things never to mind and the things to know.

Take care and mind how you go.

The Last Meeting of the Chadwick Moors Pigeon Fanciers' Association

I'm not talking about your scrubbers, even
your well-bred Northern rock dove.
Your proper racing pigeon's a Belgian:
deep throat, elastic muscle, always leading the uprush.
Sometimes when I see them all cut away from the boxes,
I think that's the whole world dematerializing,
the sky a pantomime of silk.
You see them winging first the wrong way
then exactly the right, as though a sorcerer's
apprentice made the wrong flourish
but magic itself corrected him.

> *How shall I put that in the minutes, then, like?*
> *"Bertie Highshore volunteered an ornithological rapture?"*

No, no. No rapture with the bin man rounding
the corner and the tea gone twenty minutes cold.
Our Alfie said to me, on a scale of paperback
to exoskeleton, how thin's your skin?
I'm pure carapace, me, but when he told me...
You know how it is. Time was.

When he told me he couldn't do it anymore...
> *He can't do it anymore, mind. No question.*
No, he can't, no. Have you seen
his breeding lofts? Not a right angle left

in the whole grid, just lethargy
slouching into itself. No. I know it.
On a scale of wine to vinegar, I said to him,
we know when we've turned. But

do you remember him sneaking that
sable hen with the perfect eyes into
the association house, him finally
bootlegging that bloodline? He handed
her to me when the fancier from Alnwick
stormed in and she curled against me
with the heft of a trembling eggplant.
I felt her charisma, her creature life
beating against my stillness.

On a scale of shepherd smock to
Pete Postlethwaite, call me a dreamy-
eyed rustic but I hope the last thing
I think of in this world is the sundappled moor
at the first race of the season when the
birds break out like the opening of everything
and take off, homing, into wave or particle
whatever it turns out to be   if we could get it

—or both—   get it

into the minutes,   that

                                        fugue

Miniatures

Girl, 5, Holding a Carnation.
Girl, 4, Holding an Apple.
By Isaac Oliver, 1590.

1.

Two little girls, shrunken queens,
portable as pocket-watches,
wait for their sturdy sons:

little timepieces, near-identical,
wooden-framed by manuscript "O"s.
(Oneself. Ornament. Oubliette.).

Please, what is my flower for?
this one wants to know. Why,
for your pure heart, he says.

The other says nothing, though her face
is a question. He hands her the apple
bottoms-up, the way it fell.

2.

My mother and my aunt, 7 and 9,
make the cover of the *Edmonton Journal*—
immigrant children, 1957.

One's long braids arrest him. The other,
her face a phrasebook for departure,
doesn't like his camera. (*Mister*, begs their mother,

if you take, take also my small daughter.)
He pictures both, writ round by portholes,
and the flank of the ship a blank field, white,

and I cannot help but see my mother
as the clock of her parts, antecedently me,
like Girl, 4, except her hands are free.

3.

A lady-in-waiting helps the children
off with the adamant dresses,
the velvet brocades, the nest of stays.
the collars with their tulle and framing lace,
the beaded caps, stuck pincushions
with widow's peaks in front.

What was your flower for? asks
the younger, undone and full of speech.
The older frowns and can't remember

but later under the soft down, she
drags it from the pool of hours: *Why,*
for my poor heart, she says.

Studio Animals

1. MARMOSET

> Katherine of Aragon with marmoset,
> miniature by Lucas Hornebolte

An elf at the queen's elbow, the marmoset's
too spooked for sovereignty.

Corseted in beaded mail that's both
adornment and chain, it sits

not being a small Henry while
the Queen looks away. No,

you can't help but notice how
it's almost a child. I wonder:

maybe the limner had worked up
a recipe for some periorbital pink—

some personal shade—but had to
drive it instead into a subtlety of fur

or use it to mute the beast's tender
hand, its least illumined part, monkey finger

showing where, under her clothes,
the Queen's breast, by the necklace, cleaved.

2. ERMINE

Lady with an Ermine,
Leonardo da Vinci, c. 1489-1490

A living ermine curls its warm self
on the sweet arm of the Sforza mistress:

you can see the way the hull of its belly wants
to be her lute, the way it spends

a genuine gravity. It's transverse as a
baby, it's spilled. On the far side

of their turned heads, the mutual
missing moon of their threequarter eye.

Little heraldic bloom, white forget-me-not:
she loves it. Its attention is the same

as hers, taming the same waves.
She'll bear the Duke a son, one

he'll acknowledge, so this paint narrates,
though he'll marry elsewise. *Unlikely pet,*

the oily creature, but such
a pretty animal, such a milkmaid's curl.

3. TAMARIN

Author and siblings, department store
portrait studio, 1980s

We are a seated pyramid, because there are
three of us, we are a scythe. There are only so many

ways to arrange three faces. These studio
charms, I still have them: my siblings and I

glassed in half-lockets, here descending
in a sickle along the oval frame, my brother

a slouching baby. Last night while I slept,
he was in an airplane over my city, photographing

its sunrise to show me how close we were.
I saw my sister once from a moving bus and startled

against the window. I think of marmoset and ermine
and wonder what once might have been be supplied to lie

on our depicted wrists, what animal tourniquet?
The golden lion tamarin from our Toronto zoo, the little

sparklemonkey? But we don't need a prosthetic
because we are the darlings, or we were,

when we were imprinted between conifers or against
a country gate, when we were children in a false

library, babies in a flat nursery. Lacking no
animus, we were, these charms remember, the real thing.

Only the Acupuncturist

had ever praised my tongue

*

*You have the tongue of a young
child*, she enthused, thrilled
as a nixie tube firing its cathodes,

her feisty pins in jaded places
gainsaying my insensibility

*

Cut out my tongue, I thought,
I can't find my life, or its
speculative futures

*

Was it my friend in the country,
with his lavender sprigs for my wrists,
who sang, *it's always a good year*!

or a cabaret lady in an ad
from my childhood, under
house lights, under
smoke?

The body had unbodied itself,
become a murder otter, a
naphthalene nighty

*

I remembered
a perfect black Muskoka night
with mosquitos and a ban on fires,

when I saw the complete
Milky Way, ossuary of
finished time, and

thought it was okay
to surrender to anything,

these vectors,
these small bites

*

We Have Discovered Pomegranates

In the fiftieth year of marriage, new
fruit: this chambered heart,
this *pomme-grenade*. On ice,
it's an arctic doomsday vault,
shelter-walls around seeds,
ten hopeful arils for every year

since they wed in her parents'
living room: a minidress marzipan
bungalow wedding. Rejoicing
beehives, cards *across the miles*.
Her father's camera-lighting shorted
everything, made a mid-ceremony
blackout. Flustered,

she said, "I take you, John," instead
of "I take you, James," but
it was a *sheep may safely graze*,
and a *stars will never harm you*
end of April, prairie greening,
when James was in darkness
and only moderate error taken.

Before pomegranates, they discovered
cilantro, sudoku, jazzercise
and Welsh male choirs,
boats in their stillness as a subject

for painting, weavings with fringes
like the coats of komondor dogs or
benign moonfaced monster muppets.

This aril is for Durham where, by his first home,
they discovered the cathedral doorknocker,
a lobed lionhead, arrow-dented:
centuries of fugitives pounding for entrance
while the shafts flew. They have a set
of Durham doorknocker mugs
from the year they discovered sanctuary.

And these arils are for the years
everyone started coming back home, flying
from the arrows of separate hurts
to the magnolia-hearted peace
he and she had created.
Her mother, the children, even the baby,
all growing back to themselves
in the arbor of that marriage.

Cilantro isn't a calendar, but each
capsule of pomegranate, litchi-plump,
is a canoe down a half-remembered
tributary. From the pomegranate, fat
with memory, come seeds of the nourished life:
this one a paper airplane flown from
a peak in the Rockies in 1979. That one,
a nimble animal stepping towards the hand.

You Steep

Just herbal tea while pregnant. I hate tea.
A swamp with an overtone of lemon,
the distilled bitterness of all the world's
Aunt Eglantines. To me, the seedy teabag
seems made to lurk in waystations, the rims
of sinks, the sides of plates, an alleycat
by nature, heaped on itself behind or
below the trash, drained of life, but still alive.
Thank goodness I've removed it from the brew.
I hope it won't communicate itself to you,

little one. But where are those flowering teas
I used to have? The bulb—the pearl—in a
torrent, opening and wanting touch
beyond its own capacity to touch:
rising like a quetzal, tailfeathers trailing,
and small, flocked bells courting the meniscus.
A Thumbelina petal on a bloom,
just barely there. Its name was Butterfly
Longs For Love. Spectacle. Tea caught playing,
twirling on the surface as the pool darkened,
our afternoon a Tchaikovsky sugarplum.

Kick Count

1.

Baby, you are
all surprise himalaya, giving
way to mossy avalanches,
    my flesh the breakwall
    net, the peril membrane.

2.

  How can it be
that we've never seen each
other, blind in symbiosis?
It is the strangest anguish.

3.

    We're madonna and child
      without figuration, only texture.
    No reciprocating eyes, craning for beauty,
     just the echo of ourselves in sound and space.
I'm the squish of your sourdough batch.
You're a tumble and retrieval of three or four batons.
  We'd simply never cut it as a painting.

4.
Just once,
in a black pool of translated
sound, it seemed that something
moved behind you like the nicked
tail of a turning koi. They said it was
your hair. *Your hair*! It's all I saw.
The rest of you echolocated behind a
solid fist. Baby,

5.
imagine having no face!
You're the flamingo croquet mallet
Alice handles in the garden.
I'm the plane of her experience,
I'm her palm.

Deciduous Song

In a field in California, a tree plunges
wood fingers into and through an abandoned piano—
vulgarly even, the way you'd scoop out pumpkin
gore. Keys of burnt scrimshaw, albumleaves
of leaves, and a cleaving tree almost saying
something about suffering and art

unless it's the piano that's acting on the tree,
agonizing its own felt hammers into birds
who leave it anyway, flagrant
in departure. The piano screams the tree:

the way it extrudes that heartwood-
enwrapped body reminds me
of birthing at midlife and thinking,
but now I can't die.

Clear Patrick

Clear Patrick is
a transparent boy or one
with the milky eye of a snake
about to shed its skin. He has
the look of a distance runner and
hops a little on the balls of his feet
before he begins to move. A
perfect spinning helix,
Clear Patrick is.

Clear Patrick is
a shadow puppet,
a pushpin boy with eager elbows,
loping and lolling while the light
makes a dove under his
shoulder blade. A form
on the stucco, a taker
of injury, a getter-away,
Clear Patrick is.

Clear Patrick is
a whisperer, a street
dancer, a striker of matches, a
voice in the bushes, a modern.
He's almost your son, but he's not, all
swift and strange and vulpine,
humble among honeybees
if nowhere else,
Clear Patrick is.

Mom. Clear Patrick is
that Egyptian Queen
who got bitten by an asp
and died. What's wrong with
your ears! (He falls in the street,
he's cryptic in pain, he totals
his bike, he drowns in the pool.)
Quiz me again. I'll tell you who
Clear Patrick is.

Clear Patrick is
that little boy who
slipped through the fence
and ran forever, the one who
tunnelled through stones and
out again, who lay like a monkfish, who
controlled the pace of his own heart.
He is always around, he's always
away, he's putting out lures,
he's summing you up,
Clear Patrick is.

Da Vinci Mommyblog

If I could be the tour guide of our time,
Da Vinci, I'd jockey to be the one to reveal:
humankind on the moon! and that incorruptible
footprint in a place without weather.

> *My little son loves to hear the part where*
> *the great bird—the kite—settled itself*
> *on your infant mouth as though it were*
> *a gate of entry.*

But, no, the moon is obvious. Maybe
the ocean floor is the place to start.
The lightless, nameless part of creation,
the dead sperm whale coming apart to the
nips of the metre-long sea-lice that would
be albino if the word, in that place, could mean.
These are the things we can really look upon.

> *When my son plays his Da Vinci game, he offers me parts. You*
> *can be Salai, the companion, he says, and I'll leave you*
> *the Mona Lisa when I die. Or you can be Andrea*
> *Verocchio, the teacher. Oh, but then*
> *I would have to surpass you.*
> *You can be Da Vinci's, I mean*
> *my, Mommy.*

Sorry, I digress. Photography! I want you to see
the macrophotographs of the lives of snails,
of the insides of instruments, the cello
that is otherwise a ship's cabin, the
trumpet that is otherwise a dwarven ruin.

> *He started carrying a notebook because he saw yours.*
> *He thought your anatomical drawings were inventions.*
> *He said, of the uterus, Look, I invented a place*
> *to keep folded-up babies!*
> *He stroked his chin at the scale-model of*
> *your ideal city and said, Interesting,*
> *my ideal city seems to be a*
> *city for mice!*

You should try planes, trains, funiculae.
You should go on a ferris wheel, or the Drop of Doom.
You should lose a loved possession on the tracks
and have it restored to you by a triumphant concierge.

> *I have to tell you how he cried over your brass horse, your*
> *monument to the Sforza family. As you, he considered the*
> *question of whether it could be done rearing up, at*
> *that scale. He saw it as a distraction from his*
> *research. But when the invading French*
> *fired at the clay armature, he crumpled*
> *on the floor of the gallery, crying in real life,*
> *I failed you, Sforza! Sforza, I failed!*

Modern technologies of war? I doubt you'd
find sublimity in them, despite their power.
Your tank is as quaint as a teapot
and can only move on perfectly smooth ground.
That you are an awkward imaginer
of destruction is what I love best, Da Vinci.

When he heard that they used the brass that was
meant for your equine monument instead for bullets
to repel the French, he broke. How can
something be both a horse and a bullet? he wept.
How can a bullet be made of horse?
It's okay, we said. We said, you
were a great man, Da Vinci.
He said, I died in the King
of France's arms.

Nobody on the Stair

Nobody on the stair and nobody under the lilacs.
Her child waxes solemn about the crack in the windshield,
says a time machine must have landed on the car.

Nothing but hanging lanterns, and nobody to light them.
When she was a girl during aunt-and-uncle summer nights
she'd run at that one flowerbed and launch and sail

and plant her feet, little prods to the ground's mossy palate.
Not long jump or high jump or triple jump, but *night* jump,
the best of the jumps: it proved that her body worked,

that it appreciated even in darkness the peegee hydrangea,
that it had natural clearance. Do you remember her flying school?
No, you don't. None of its graduates really kept in touch,

and now there's nobody to notice the golden drinking cup.
It's not golden, anyway, it's peach blush. *Don't give her that old mug*,
her father-in-law had said, years ago, nervous when she was new.

But her husband had answered, *This is your best cup, Dad. A Fire King
in a rare colour. Peach blush*. This one she's holding now's a copy,
bought from an antique store. It had been serving other mouths.

Nobody left to be her husband's mother. No back-to-the-house-
for-potato-salad again. She jumps over the Queen Anne's Lace
in the front garden: the kind that draws, in other seasons, bees.

Nobody left to be her husband's father. Her husband has been,
for these few years, the Dad. He has a knee-bounce for toddlers that he calls
The Paint Can. She jumps over the rock garden once, and once again.

Nobody to notice the child choose his colours. *A Hallowe'en painting*!
he says, and the water, murky, swirls. She and her husband
are shocked to be at the forefront. No, she thinks, there's nobody on the stair

where the lift had lately held her husband's mother, where the chair
had borne her up and down again. The child is holding out his spooky pictu
I used dead paint, he says, and hopes she's scared.

Tilt-Shift

A subplot to a subplot to a subplot
in this corner of Lego New York
in a nether grotto of my own basement:

a cop standing behind a mime, dire,
the cuffed mime lurching as he's led away.
The heart of his repertoire is the unjointed body.

He didn't have a permit! He got busted.
(My child holds no truck with unlicensed busking,
and has cross-pollinated his little sets to prove it.)

A painted teardrop on a plastic cheek.
Should I care, I wonder, if he is shaping up
to be a punisher of bureaucratic transgressions

that go down in tiny worlds?

                    What's the name
of that miniaturizing lens? It makes toys
of everything, candy-saturated.

                    When I was small, I had

a bus-conductor's kit, confesses my father.
I issued tickets.

Me too, I say, I *rubber-stamped*
the papers on a hundred local dogs while

Grandma's clock sang on the mantel.
You can't have alienated hounds, my
urge was to license. My son says:

If you are not afraid of maned wolves,
dungeons, lava, nosewhistling witches, tidal waves,
cracks in the pavement, poison snakes, sign here.

The children are mayoral over dogcatchers,
superintendent over landlords. They are the parks
officers of quicksand. They are the consulting
surgeons of bubblegum choking the heart.

Dog Days with Borrowed Dog

i.m. Frida

Little housewolf, your son composes. *Bone   ball   disc.*
Leery ambler, she won't walk when the dark is settling.

She runs from the cannons of summer symphonies,
from the fireworks the boy calls *poppingstars.*

She isn't your animal: you tend her as a nun
tends a convent garden. But if you fall in step, she'll

let you feel the bright quills of her ancestral aversions. *How can
a four-footed creature walk in dactyls?* Your energy

and your custom are hers to determine. *One foot must be
a ghost foot.* You walk with a ghost foot: her gift. Your heart

is a mallet on a carnival strength test, your arms twigs
in which other twigs reside. She only wants to know what kind

of arc will come from the bone-ball-disc that lately
extended you. Your first throw is a rusty junket

without a terminus. But in your aspiring arm lies the parabola
so well described that it trails sparklers from itself,

masking whatever's left of August and still to come of night.
You dote too openly. Each fetch is a figure eight.

Crossroads

His eye a keyhole
to nobody's
amber sunroom,

the prairie hare
sits deep
in the neglected lot

we pass in the evenings.
His ears
de-tulip at our approach

and Victor sighs
thank you.
I ask him why

he thanked the rabbit—
baby Vic,
who has no more years of life

than he has feet,
and whose
eyes are steadfast

when he says,
for noticing me.
Leaving, the wind

puffs seed
pods loose
to pepper our shoes.

For It is Not the Same River
and We are Not the Same

The year I promised you no two baths alike,
we nightly invented new terms for day's dissolution.

Ice cube toy bath: captive figures melting
out of the ice cubes and into the flows.

Jellyfish bath: the plastic pudding cups
we kept for paint pots inching towards you

on capillary waves as you tittered, their
imaginary sting a vivid prospect. Bath-

in-the-dark, in the thickening dark, just that.
Ceiling-abseiling papery butterflies

utterly falling for you: butterfly bath.
Targets I tagged on a shower curtain,

splat of your water-balloons: lawn-game bath.
I admonished you once for flooding the room,

pressing your foot flat against the faucet,
making a plate-balancer's plate of water.

I'm sorry, you said, *but I did love the effect of it.*
Your "sorry" was a trill in a glade. I heard "did love"

in the Renaissance way. You cried during umbrella-
in-the-shower bath, its nerve-end tin-roof patter.

Now it's quarantine year, and you turn twelve.
Tall, private, full of headphones. My drive

to show one day's difference from another,
gone. Our knack for making worlds within our walls,

gone. You keep your own hours, up all night.
When morning comes in at the smudged window,

our fingerprints throw light everywhere, wash out
our whole experience. Yet I remember a green bath,

a snowball bath, a starts-with-B bath: alliterative broth
of bowls, bubbles and brachiosauruses,

where a beater chewed the water
as though it were addressing itself

to the most anemic egg. And ebullient you,
whipping up whirlpools, both riddle and force.

Rowan, We Are Ordinary—

for my son

ordinary in the knot of time, under the powder moon,
        in the redolent grass;
ordinary in the uncanny houses, the dreamed ones with the mahogany
        and the moving swells under the rug;
ordinary to the indifferent eyes of the faster animals
        and the more vigilant ones; ordinary, but in reckless camouflage;
ordinary on the plains, ordinary in the forests, ordinary
        in the more or less riddled pathways of light.

Once I raised a stone against a fish (under the bridge near school
        they congregated darkly) and my best friend stayed my hand.
        I don't know why I did it.
Once my grandmother cupped my face in her palms
        and called me an angel. No—many times. I said "once"
        because the mercy of the kitchen was entire.
Once I came down a wide stair and everyone I knew was standing before
Once I cried until I was insincere, then laughed my way back from it.
        Have you ever done that?

We are ordinary. Oh, Rowan. We are ordinary.

Sometimes we said you were named for a tree:
        the mountain ash, the rowan tree.
Sometimes we said you were named for a British comedian.
Sometimes we asked ourselves whether it had become
        more of a girl's name, whether it mattered.

Divining; that was what the rowan branch was for. And the British
          comedian had a certain legerdemain.

Somewhere I read that, as a matter of cognition, we assume
          covered objects to be perfect. You, for example,
          when you were inside and undercover,
            once kicked a volume right off my belly, right through all the veils.
I was reading Gwendolyn MacEwen (*now there are no bonds except the flesh*),
          about a boy escape artist.
In a world you could not intuit, you moved an object. What was not possible?

Wherever you live now, I tell you this because
          I know you'll forget: we are ordinary.

Rowan, we are ordinary in the scattering days, ordinary
          in the leaf museum, ordinary in the giant lexicon of the world;
ordinary in the rake of the horizon and in the terminals of sight.
In the disposition of the stars, we are ordinary.
We were ordinary in the potential of your first homecoming. You had
          forgotten your ninepound self in some ordinary way
            and were asleep. Dusty Springfield sang you to where you were going.
Parallel lines converged, and it was seasonally average weather.

Your father's hands were shaking at the wheel.

This Dark Cinema

In this dark cinema (*Thor:
Ragnarok*), I'm staring at Odin's
rosegold eyepatch

when my son mentions
the pet dog he left
in my womb.

Who's been feeding this dog,
I ask my child, *these seven years
since you've been gone?*

Odin and his sons together
under an olive sky traverse
a field pale as a Chernobyl

ghostmall's gasmask fretwork.
—*Nobody!
Nobody was feeding the dog!*

*And that's why the womb
requested my brother.
That's actually how you got pregnant.*

Odin and his offspring
pause where the field meets
the bluff. The field

greets the sea and asks it
where the limit is, of generation.
Also: what's under the eyepatch?

—dead zone, war zone,
tent city, papers, passes,
careening oil pelican and

plastic midnight ocean,
captive masses, burning, burning
rare and precious canopy.

What if it costs an eye to learn
that it takes both eyes
to see?

At least, I tell myself,
my two sons will have cared in common
for the same creature,

one thing pulled back
from the edge of the feral.

Thanks for My Son's Innocent Knees, and Thanks

for the suction in the library door that
lets me think I'm a muscular reader, and thanks
for letting me open my eyes this time and the next.

Also, going back: for the way one grandmother sang in that
Coronation Street postwar brass kind of way, and the way
 the other one sucked the air through pursed lips for focus;
for the way my dad whistled through his teeth and
for my mom's hoarse cough when she drew
the morning curtain. Thanks for the way the air
went in and out of all of them. And

for that secret place in the forest where the creek ran under ice,
for the park my grandfather wouldn't let me go to, for the rush
of the winging bats, the T-bar I fell off, the horse that kicked me, the
reprimand from the lifeguard. Thanks for the things
of my own making that I tore
apart, smaller and
smaller,
for the night I failed as my brother's
tooth fairy, for the day I dressed up
to meet my newborn nephew.
Are you... wearing makeup?
my sister asked. *For the baby?*

Thanks for the performance of *Ruddigore* where I
resolved to hold his hand and for how it wasn't
too late even after the intermission, and
for when he kissed me in the Peel subway, over
the turnstile, crowdstopping. I had to recall
a pop-art Peter Parker and Mary Jane just to
know, like a dance step, where my hands should
be: there's *no time*, in a turnstile kiss, so
thanks. Thanks, even,

for the night when, so much later, my mother-in-law dying,
I walked into the night-street marvelling
at the operation of my own body, the leaves
going to the very places where my toes pushed them, and
the excoriating light coming from that one lamp,

the cars like barges on a sea of gold
in the misty season with its fire pit air
and for the permeable way it all finally
happened to sink in.

Train

Bales: like fifty firm decisions
the land itself has made.
Passable as minutes.
I will admit to liking them

but those prolific purple flowers
militant on the hill
are the real arrest,
impress me with the hour's density

especially for the ground they give
the ruined tree, its three
prongs, its crows all
shipwrecked to a great vitality.

Right now I am sure the evening
resists us, that we ourselves
are hauling in its striations,
motion alone making the world.

Slowing, I worry: every last thing
held firmly up to notice may
be empty in its own disclosure,
the static anthem of itself.

Once someone asked me to see
the likeness of Rasputin
whorled into his cat's ear,
what did I think it meant?

In Brockville the train shunts
back and forth, an understudy to itself,
neither coming nor going, so perfect
in its adequacy that I finish this, smiling.

**Ladies and gentlemen,
I have no information.
When I have information,
I will keep you informed.**

"The Tilled Field" is poem is based on the 1923 painting by Joan Miró.

"Elisabeth" includes a line by Russian playwright Anton Chekhov written in an 1887 letter to M.V. Kisilev: "A litterateur is not a confectioner." The reference may be found in *Letters on the Short Story, The Drama, and Other Literary Topics*, edited by Louis S. Friedland (New York, 1924), p. 275.

Biographical elements and italicized quotations in "Ludwig Koch's Library" come from Ludwig Koch's memoir, *Memoirs of a Birdman*, published by Phoenix House (London) in 1955. The last phrase, *Who cooks for you?*, while italicized, is not from Koch's memoir, but represents internalized speech.

"Poison Garden" was written after a visit to Alnwick in 2013. I was entranced by the notion of a poison garden, though it was closed when I visited. The materials for this poem were furnished by a visit to the castle and an imagined walk through a poison garden.

I accessed these images in "Newcastle Criminal Gallery, 1871-1873": through a Flickr collection. In order to emphasize the fictional quality of my imagining of them, I changed the first names of all the photographed subjects.

"The Last Meeting of the Chadwick Moors Pigeon Fanciers' Assocation": This association does not exist, nor does the location of Chadwick Moors. I learned quite a lot about pigeon-fancying from the 2009 documentary *Little Ripper*, directed by Craig Boord and Jarrod Boord.

The inset lyric in "Only The Acupuncturist" alludes to a commercial by Hochtaler Wines.

"We Have Discovered Pomegranates" is dedicated to my mother and father, married April 30, 1970.

The description of the tree and the piano in "Deciduous Song" alludes to an art installation in California, "Piano Tree," by Jeff Mifflin.

"Clear Patrick" was inspired by Elizabeth Bishop's poem "Man-Moth."

"Da Vinci Mommyblog" makes reference to the BBC documentary Planet Earth, and alludes to the photographs of Vyacheslav Mishchenko and Björn Ewers. It also derives from the many, indeed weekly, visits my family paid to the Da Vinci exhibit at the Saskatchewan Science Centre in the spring of 2013.

"Rowan, We are Ordinary" cites Gwendolyn MacEwen's poem, "Manzini," which was first published in *A Breakfast for Barbarians* in 1966.

The title of "For It is Not the Same River and We Are Not the Same" alludes to the Greek philosopher Heraclitus's notion of fluid time: "No man ever steps in the same river twice, for it's not the same river and he's not the same man."

"Thanks for My Son's Innocent Knees, and Thanks" makes references to the Gilbert and Sullivan opera, Ruddigore, and to characters from The Amazing Spider-Man comic by Stan Lee.

ACKNOWLEDGEMENTS

Some of these poems have previously appeared in *Arc Poetry Magazine*, *Room*, *Event*, *Contemporary Verse 2*, *The Malahat Review*, *The Fiddlehead*, and *Grain*, as well as in Tightrope Press's *Best Canadian Poetry* (2012) and the Saskatchewan Writers' Guild's pandemic anthology. I would like to thank the editors of those journals and anthologies. Thanks to Kelley Jo Burke for producing and performing several of these poems for CBC Radio's *Sound Xchange* and to Susan Gillis for interviewing me on her literary blog, *Concrete and River*.

I am very grateful to Carmine Starnino for his long support and for his discerning editing of this book. Thank you to Simon Dardick and Véhicule Press, and to David Drummond for the ingenious cover design.

I feel very fortunate to have benefitted from the warmth and excellence of the writing community cultivated by the Saskatchewan Writers' Guild. I thank the Guild and the City of Regina for helping to fund this work through the City of Regina Writing Award in 2015.

I owe a giant and most affectionate thank you to my writing group, the Poets out of the Vault (POV): Troni Grande, Kathleen Wall, Michael Trussler, Jes Battis, Melanie Schnell, Tracy Hamon, Tara-Dawn Solheim and Sheri Benning.

Some of these poems were written with mentorship from Richard Sanger, Stephanie Bolster, Hoa Nguyen and Elizabeth Phillips, for which I am very thankful. I am most grateful, as well, for everything I have learned about poetry from Brian Trehearne.

It has been a great privilege to have been able to write this book in dialogue with my wonderful colleagues and students in the English Department at the University of Regina. Many dear friends have supported this book, as well as many fine writers whose own work I've experienced as a great gift.

Thanks to Helen Kuk, Gord Sellar, Matt Huculak and Lara Stoudt for writing with me. Thanks to Amanda Quibell, Keira Travis and Julia Saric for living with my projects. Thank you to my friend Shelley Boyd for all her enthusiasm for this manuscript and for the many kicks in the pants.

I'm deeply indebted to my family for the creation of this book, not only because it was sustained by their unconditional love and indulgence, but because it is permeated by their voices. Thanks to my husband Mark Lajoie for his companionship and his contributions to this book. Thanks to my son Rowan, whose wonderful insights are all over this book's later pages, and whose phrase gave *Little Housewolf* its title. Thanks to my son Victor, for the perpetual sweet surprise of his imagination and nature. Love and thanks to my parents, Jim and Helga Purdham, and my siblings Alexis and Sean Spisani and Daniel and Adelle Purdham and their families, for all our shared adventures. Love and thanks to Christa Freiler and David Thornley, Erich Freiler and Lindsey Reed, Elisabeth and the late Wolfgang Freiler and their families, as well as to the late Maureen and Sonny Calland, Gwen Park and the late Alby Park, the late Emily and John Wardle, and David and June Purdham and their families.

In loving memory of my in-laws, Marlyn and Donnie Lajoie, and Pat Weatherhead. Love and thanks to Jen Weatherhead and family, to Robin Ganev and Jeet Heer and family, and to Andrea, Norma and Doug Brown.

In loving memory of my cherished grandparents, Margarete and Herbert Freiler and Gladys and James Purdham.

CARMINE STARNINO, EDITOR

MICHAEL HARRIS, FOUNDING EDITOR

Robert Allen • James Arthur • John Asfour, trans.
Doug Beardsley • Paul Bélanger • Linda Besner
Walid Bitar • Marie-Claire Blais • Yves Boisvert
Asa Boxer • Susan Briscoe • René Brisebois, trans.
Mark Callanan • Chad Campbell • Edward Carson
Arthur Clark • Don Coles • Vincent Colistro
Jan Conn • Geoffrey Cook • Lissa Cowan, trans
Judith Cowan, trans. • Mary Dalton • Ann Diamond
George Ellenbogen • Louise Fabiani •Joe Fiorito
Bill Furey • Michel Garneau • Susan Glickman
Gérald Godin • Richard Greene • Jason Guriel
Michael Harris • Carla Hartsfield • Elisabeth Harvor
Charlotte Hussey • Dean Irvine, ed. • D.G. Jones
Anita Lahey • Kateri Lanthier • Ross Leckie
Michael Lista • Laura Lush • Errol MacDonald
Brent MacLaine • Muhammad al-Maghut
Nyla Matuk • Robert McGee, trans. • Sadiqa Meijer
Robert Melançon • Robert Moore • Pierre Morency
Pierre Nepveu • Eric Ormsby • Elise Partridge
Christopher Patton • Michael Prior • Medrie Purdham
John Reibetanz • Peter Richardson • Robin Richardson
Laura Ritland • Talya Rubin • Richard Sanger
Stephen Scobie • Peter Dale Scott • Deena Kara Shaffer
Carmine Starnino • Andrew Steinmetz • David Solway

Ricardo Sternberg • Shannon Stewart
Philip Stratford, trans. • Matthew Sweeney
Harry Thurston • Rhea Tregebov • Peter Van Toorn
Patrick Warner • Derek Webster • Anne Wilkinson
Donald Winkler, trans. • Shoshanna Wingate
Christopher Wiseman • Catriona Wright
Terence Young